In the Woods

An Adventure Friends Story

By Amy Hartman

BZZZZZZZZZZ

Lindsey is working hard, and-
BZZZZZZZZZZ

-noisily.

"Are you almost done with that new gadget?"
says Twit, the Kinkas bird, in a voice that sounds like
Star, the Singtata.
"If not, then hurry up, tuts!"

"You never call me tuts, Star," says Lindsey. "Just a small minute."
Star can't help giggling. Twits sounds like he is trying to tease Star, but he made her sound cool, and Star likes that. And it was funny.

"Let's hope she doesn't make a robot rain-cloud," says Momo.

"Why?" Asks Star

"Because I will be moving it around when one room gets too wet, unless she make a remote and wheels to go with it.

"Done!" Says Lindsey

"So, it's not a cloud?" asks Momo. "No," says Lindsey. "It's a Wood Wanderer!"

Lindsey just finished making the WW and is ready to drive it out.

"Let's go!" She calls.

"Where?" asks Star

"Into the woods!" Lindsey answers

"Oh, right. That makes sense," says Star

VRRRRRMMM--KRRRRTCH-VRRM
KRTCH-KRTCH-VRRRRRRM

"What's that sound?" Asks Momo

It's the e-e-e-e-ngi-i-i-in" says Lindsey. "The road is very rocky and bumpy."

"Stay low," Lindsey says.

"Why?" Asks Twit. Suddenly the car bumps over a large rock and everyone squeals in surprise.

"See?" Says Lindsey.

"Yeah, got it. Stay low."

THUMP! BANG! CRASH!!

"What's that?" asks Star.

"A fight," Lindsey replies.

"Uh-oh," says Momo.

A forentick, an evil snake-looking forest spirit, was attacking a legendary Forestine, a spirit protector of the woods. It was not going well for the Forestine.

"We've got to help the turtle!" Says Star.
"Yes," Momo agrees, "we have to help!"

"Yes," says a mysterious voice. "If the forestine is defeated, the Forentick will take over the forest, and that's very bad."

A Mynsonia steps into view as they speak.

"Who are you?" Asks Lindsey.

"My nam,e is Mynti," says the Mynsonia. "I can predict the future, and I have an idea that can help."

"Let's hear it," Momo says.

"Gather the deer, racoons, foxes, and wolves. Put them behind the snake and the creatures will ambush it. This will give the Forestine a chance to defend against the Forentick."

The plan worked! All the animals gathered surprised the forentick, and the Forestine was able to defend itself agains the attack. The Forentick slithered away in fear and the forest was safe.

"Mynti, would you like to go
on more adventures with us?"
Star asks.

"I think that would be lots of
fun!" Mynti says. "I would
love to join your team!"

"Twit twit TWIIIT"
says Twit.

"Welcome! We're happy to
have you," Lindsey says.

Thank you for reading my third
published book!

By Amy Hartman